Songs of Tribute
Poems
by
Oliver Allen
2020

Poems

## Songs of Tribute

As a small speck of cosmic dust
In this Einstein universe
I am humbled everytime
I step outside
From the corner of my world
I have so many questions
About the way things are
And the way things are started
These questions I have
I keep buried in my head
Unless I allow them to be read
I swallow my pride
Everytime I go outside
Into this vastly astrophysical world.

I owe alot of my good nature
To the books I've read
Over the years, many fears
Have allowed me to be mislead
But when I get back on track
I try to move forward
And not look back...

If you were to join me
In a quest to find ourselves
You would see that I am humbled
And have nothing but appreciation
For this entire encapsulation
Of every blade of grass
Of every bumble bee
Of every drop of rain
Of every flower bed that has weeds
Inside God's infinitely creative mind

Yes, I make mistakes sometimes
I'm not perfect but I try my best
To question and not protest
Evolution or change
But as things mitigate
I am changing too
As we all are these days
As we all are these days

As we all are these days

So as a method to understand you
You, who is reading this preview
Of a sentiment of my life's duel
With the better half and worse too

These are my Songs of Tribute
These are my Songs of Tribute
These are my Songs of Tribute

To everything in my life.

O.A.

## Canada Day

United we stand
On this celebratory day
July 1, is Canada's birthday
Let us rejoice in our freedom
Let us rejoice in our Constitution
That united the 3 separate colonies:
Canada, Nova Scotia, and New Brunswick
Into a single Dominion
With the colony of Canada
Expanding into Quebec and Ontario

Let us rejoice with carnivals
Let us rejoice with festivals
Let us rejoice in our multiculturalism
Let us rejoice in our Dominion
Giving us our independence

As an independently formed British Colony
Many different people call this home
Many different cultures are in these zones
The 10 provinces and 3 territories
House all types of folks
And they are proud of this country inside
They showcase their national pride
Each year with parades
Each year with barbeques
And each year with fireworks and lights

So let us rejoice in our freedom
Let us rejoice in our Constitution
That united the 3 separate colonies:
Canada, Nova Scotia, and New Brunswick
Into a single Dominion:

Happy Canada Day!

O.A.

## Love Can Move Mountains

Come away with me, take my hand
Take my hand
I just might be a poet
But I can paint a picturesque world
With words, if you give me a chance;
Through the fire and rain, sleet and hail
Through underwater caverns, sea trails
Through desert storms, island waterways
Through mountain skylines, passageways
I can take you through it all, if you give me
Give me a chance to turn on the lights
You'll never be lonely again in your life
Mother I love you in this momentous night
Mother I give you every ounce of my life
I will open your imagination tonight
I will open your imagination tonight

Love can move mountains
Love can save the world
Love can be so wonderful
If people open their minds to its powers
For every person Love can be
The greatest thing on Earth
For every person Love can be
The greatest thing on Earth

Come away with me, take my hand
Run as fast as you can
I just might be a dreamer
But I can paint a picturesque world
With words, if you give me a chance;
It's up to you, where you'd like to go
It's a cold world, but no need to be alone
It's a trying time for people, don't you know
But in this world, I won't ever let you go
I can take you through it all, if you give me
Give me a chance to turn on the lights
You'll never be lonely again in your life
Mother I love you in this momentous night
Mother I give you every ounce of my life
I will open your imagination tonight
I will open your imagination tonight

Love can move mountains
Love can save the world
Love can be so wonderful
If people open their minds to its powers
For every person Love can be
The greatest thing on Earth
For every person Love can be
The greatest thing on Earth

I can take you through it all, if you give me
Give me a chance to turn on the lights
You'll never be lonely again in your life
Mother I love you in this momentous night
Mother I give you every ounce of my life
I will open your imagination tonight
I will open your imagination tonight

Love can move mountains
Love can save the world
Love can be so wonderful
If people open their minds to its powers
For every person Love can be
The greatest thing on Earth
For every person Love can be
The greatest thing on Earth

O.A.

## The Space Beyond

Staring into blank space...
The dark vespers of a multitude of stars
The vortex of astronomical opaqueness
The swirling cosmic influx of dust particles
The debris of mindfull progression
Of a universe ever vastly expanding
From the cinderblock of a Big Bang
Cascading below and above the twilight
Twilight of a juxstapositioned orbiting
        Sun and Moon
        Earth and Clouds
        Blackhole and Comet

We witness the greatness of creation
Within our universe of deposition
And we are humbled
Ever so humbled
By God's infinite touch
The wand of which is weilded daily;
And as a solitary man
I sit and wonder
How and why God loves us
So much?
How and why God gives us
So much?
This is what I have wondered
Everyday
Growing
Up.

O.A.

## Molecules

Symbiotic nature of things
Skeletons with bone density
Saturated with atomic molecules
Redefines the universal definition
Of colliding into you

We are just flesh and blood
We are just a tombstone away
From an arrangement with God
Redefining the universal definition
Of redirecting you

We are just atomic molecules
We are just the sun and moon
For every day that we rule
Redefines the universal definition
Of me loving you

We are just human beings
We are just looking for meaning
Farther out in the world
Redefining the universal definition
Of us getting through

We are just atomic molecules
We are just atomic molecules
We are just atomic molecules
What can we do?
What can we do?

O.A.

### To Jonathan Larson

I love what you did
With your time here on Earth
Making a strong contribution
Not just to A.M.T.
But to theater around the world
You were living on borrowed time
But you still found a way to shine
I heard you read the newspaper
Every day of your theatrical life
And I saw RENT more than twice
I saw RENT more than twice
Mimi was my favorite character
She was nice.
Life.

O.A.

## Unrequited Love

For the Librarians who discouraged me:

This was the title of my very 1st poem
I wrote
Back in high school for a contest -
When I went to the library
After basketball practise
The school librarians
Were laughing at my submission.
It was full of Gobbley Gook
And did not make much sense;
And after being upset
I vowed to never write again.
I never told anyone about that contest
After basketball practise
But luckily, I continued writing.

I don't expect to ever be a poet laureate
Or even expect to get published one day
But writing and self expression has been my passion
Since a very young age.
Since a very young age.

O.A.

## It's a Lovely Day

It's a perfect day to handle you
You've been a thorn in my side
For too long
Wake up
I've felt betrayed by our song
Your nimble deceit has projected
A sense of mistrust all along
They say when you write hard,
Especially a poem, you become
The person you really are...
So I will Zen fold myself
And as my better half
And better self would do
I will take you from
The start...

O.A.

## To My Guardian

I know who you are
I've seen your face in my dreams
I am sorry I could not save you
From your journey
From your journey

How is it on the other side?
Is it as warm as a summer breeze?
Are there pillars of clouds without end?
Does it rain with joy and sunshine endlessly?
I only want to know these things
To know how you're doing

These days because of you I'm alright
I try to make the world as bright
Without you

These days in every way I see your light
Illuminating every lamp post as I walk by
Because that is what you do
You make my world brighter
You make my world tighter
You know I've always been a writer
And I see you are trying to be kinder
By being there for me
By giving me what I need
Indeed
Indeed

You and me.

O.A.

## I'm No Good to You Anymore

I'm no good to you anymore
I'm a drunk that's fuck up
See me lying here on your floor?
Baby, I'm no good to you anymore

What do you want from me?
Can't you see I have tendencies?
I only want you to leave through the door
Baby, I'm no good to you anymore

If you think I'm going to change
Think again my little friend
I only want you to love me and don't be sore
Baby, I'm no good to you anymore

Baby, I'm no good to you anymore
Baby, I'm no good to you anymore
Baby, I'm no good to you anymore
Baby, I can't get up off the floor.

O.A.

**Down the Rabbit Hole**

Down the rabbit hole we go
Down the rabbit hole we go
Where we'll end up
Where we'll end up
No one knows
No one knows

If you dislike mice
Then you should think twice
Because we're going into a burrow
That extends quite awhile just so you know.
In case we should run into a thing or two
With many eyes, and feet playing a sleuth
Weather the storm by caving in the truth.

Down the rabbit hole we go
Down the rabbit hole we go
Where we'll end up
Where we'll end up
No one knows
No one knows

Down the rabbit hole we go
Down the rabbit hole we go
Where we'll end up
Where we'll end up
No one knows
No one knows

I see a monster with green fur and eyes
Yellow is it's tail to my surprise
Do you see it too? Or recognize it?
How it evades us without our trust
I only can imagine
How many people it's been catching
Over the years
With many tears from little children
With their fears.

Down the rabbit hole we go
Down the rabbit hole we go
Where we'll end up

Where we'll end up
No one knows
No one knows

Down the rabbit hole we go
Down the rabbit hole we go
Where we'll end up
Where we'll end up
No one knows
No one knows

However, these kinds of things
Don't exist in real existing
But are rather made up
To stop you from climbing
Down a rabbit hole
To see what your imagination
Brings you in the end
Of a great silly story re-imagined.

Down the rabbit hole we go
Down the rabbit hole we go
Where we'll end up
Where we'll end up
No one knows
No one knows

Down the rabbit hole we go
Down the rabbit hole we go
Where we'll end up
Where we'll end up
No one knows
No one knows

O.A.

## Time Well Spent

You love
I love
You fold
I fold
You break
I break
You grow old
I grow old
You have a heart attack
I have a heart attack
Parrallel Lives
Parrallel Lives
This is what I see in your eyes
This is what I see in your eyes
Over time
Over time

O.A.

## What a Poem is Not

A poem doesn't have to mean anything
Poetry 101
A poem just "is."

But what a poem is not:
A confession
An excuse
A vehicle for emotion
Unless it's kinetic.

What a poem is not:
An advertisement
An excuse for others to imitate
Unless the words
Reverberate.

What a poem is not:
Is a set of lyrics
Is a predictable form
Unless it has shape
Or is set to music.

A poem is an idea
Or self expression
A subjective
Or objective
Question or conclusion -
Or just thing.

O.A.

## Timecapsule

I cannot tell anyone
I do not want to be discovered
Untill the year 4034
My soul I buried years ago
Like a madman shoveling
My way into history
Mystery is, where did I hide it?
My soul in the muearth
My hands filthy with dirt
I have felt guilty all along
What if I'm not that good
Many years carried along?
What if my timecapsule
Belongs up on Mars?
With all those spacecars?
Who is to say what is good
And what needs to be down?
All I know is that I buried
My soul, a long time ago...

Who is to say what is good
And what needs to be down?
All I know is that I buried
My soul, a long time ago...

O.A.

## Silence

Blank page, blank face
Eyes closed, eyes closed
Exceptional silence
Nothingness

Samuri posture
Sword drawn
Before dawn
Nothingness

I will not break
I will not bend
But rescindicate
My means to an end

I finally have the block
The terrible block
Silence
Nothingness
Nothingness
So as a samuri
Sword drawn
I will do as a samuri does
When you have betrayed your heart
What we do to create and make art.
Silence.

O.A.

## My Illicit Muse

Inspiration is everywhere
If you stop to breath
And take in the beautiful sites
A sunflower blooms
In every corner
Of this incubating world...
For every red rose
There's a daffodil that grows
The garden of life is plentiful
Allowing all kinds of room
For everything to bloom...
But for me, my muse
Is seeing and experiencing
The exceptional feeling
Of everything that succeeds
When I think of my muse
There's beauty in practising
What successful people preach.
A rose is not a rose
Unless it knows -
Confidence
In what you are
Is so important.

O.A.

## Defenders of Saint Jude's Music School

In the year 2037
In a post apocalyptic world
Cities were destroyed
In the meteor shower
And flash floods
Leaving towns desolate.
While parents rebuilt
Institutions of work
Children of the New Order
Had nowhere to reside
Except in schools inside.
Teachers had no idea
What to teach them
Because the world they knew
Had come to an end;
So they had lesson plans
That involved learning
To play an instrument
Learning the value
Of music.

However, as the world changed
So did the way students played
Their newfound instruments.
The Children of the New Order
Found magic in the music learned -
And at one school run by:
A Saint named Judith Nigh
The children earned the right
To mix music with magic inside.
The school was on the westcoast
In a little town called Nanaimo
And everyday the children played
With music in their own way...

One of the children
Was beside themselves
When she was banging
On some pots and pans
And a fire started
In her tiny hands...

A 15 year old girl
Named Bethany Wegale
Turned to Saint Jude
And asked in music history class
Is this true?
Mixing magic with music
Bends the physics rules?
Saint Jude explained
To the Children of the New Order
Rhythms and certain chords
Make the magic set sail...
Saint Jude demonstrated
In the foray
Of her Music School
Sitting in a circle round;
She began clapping
A certain musical phrase
Closing her eyes sound...

To the children's surprise
A couple birds appeared
Out of her gloves
When Bethany and the others
Looked, there were 2 doves!!
This made Bethany
Practise her scales
When she returned home
After a long, long day...

Her Mother Miss Wegale
Made sure she practised
Every night of the week
Augmented, diminished
And even chromatic
Miss Wegale made sure
She practised, so one day
She could do magic.

The next day,
Bethany went to school
And blew everyone away
With what she knew.
She made a hat dissappear
And fire light up her back

In clapping some syncopated
Rhythms all the way through.
Saint Jude was proud
So she made everyone
Clap some rhythms outloud
Under the open lit sun.
As they sat outside
In the deserted courtyard
Filled with garbage and strife
A few students gave the sign
That they wanted to improve
On what they already knew...

In the circle round
A student started to play
Play the violin
And the other students
Began to listen.
Another student joined in
And began to sing
Another student started
To play the cello
And then something bellowed;
In the middle
Of the circle round
A swirling tower of fire
Sparked up from the ground...
Seeing this Saint Judith
Suddenly exclaimed:
"See students, this is the power
Of music mixed with magic;
You can ward off anything
Or anyone, if you have it..."

As Saint Judith was praising
The Children of the New Order
In the circle round,
Listening to their music
And watching their fire blaze down
From behind her
Sneaking up almost as quiet
As a sneaky foul mouse
A student from another tribe
Another student from another school

Came up to Saint Jude
And asked her if she ran this institution?
Saint Judith replied:
"Yes! This is my Music School!
Who the Hell, my child, are you!?"

"We are from the Balta Music School
From the other side of the Island
My school and I want to break your circle
Your song cycle of our deserted lands...
Let us battle to see who sings the best!
Let us battle to see who plays the best!
Let us battle to see who can make music
And empower the best Music School
Our teacher is on her way now..."

Saint Judith looked behind her
Past the foreign student
And there was a tribe of others
Not much older than her children
But the assertion had burned through.

Without further ado,
Bethany and her fellow students
Belted out a mantra to not lose:

"Defend the circle!
Defend our round!
Sing with power!
And turn them inside out..."
The chants were ear piercing
And the battle begun...

Each side sang with fury
Clapping rhythms like dominoes
Creating pillars and towers of fire
The magic crescendoing in a symphony of chaos.
Saint Judith battled the Balta Teacher
With her Mozart imitation Magic Flute
And the students from both schools
Gathered to watch them duel
One student from Saint Jude's
Pushed the Balta Teacher too

Saint Judith finally played
A set of notes
That had the Balta Teacher
By the rope.
It was the beginning of the end
Of the Balta Music Teacher
Because with her Magic Flute
Saint Judith set her hair on fire..

"Don't you come back here!
Ever no more" she claimed,
"Take your students
And be gone!"

The Balta Music Teacher
Holding her head, motioned
For her students to retreat
And indeed they did -
Back to the streets.

Bethany looked to Saint Judith
And her fellow students joined in
Singing, clapping and playing
Their instruments...

For years onward,
Saint Jude's Music School
Would survive
As things in the world
Moved on and died.
Music was something
Each child learned
And helped shape the foundation
Of a new creative world.
The Children of the New Order
Would grow up and bring magic
To each of their own
Making learning music a priority
Over the years,
In their homes.

O.A.

## Aptitude

There once was a child
With a high IQ
People used to wonder
What happened to you?

Were you dropped as an infant?
Were you left out in the cold?
How do you know so much?
And think of so much stuff?

Being smart was cool
But one day he dropped out of school

"Too bad," said one
"Too bad," said another
He didn't want to be bothered
So he played dumb
Dumb and dumber

But little did he know
He would grow
And self-teach himself
Into self-help
And go back to night school

Where he met a teacher that was cool
And explained the golden rule
No matter what people say
You do you
And have it
No other way

That kid became a Doctor
Because of what that teacher
Told him to his face
A high IQ
Almost got in his way
But he saved his life
And that's what I wanted to say:

Don't put the blame on you
To be blamed.

Aptitude is a blessing
Not a disgrace.

O.A.

## Ballad of the All-inclusive

In this circle
In this round
There are things
That you may not touch

If you break
If you disrupt
This chain of command
You might not understand

If you don't ask
If you don't ask nicely
Then the circle won't open
And let you in for therapy

Inclusiveness
And all its outs and ins
Are part of the system here
And you want to be included

You want to be
You want to be
With everyone else
On the other side of the rainbow

Looking for that pot
Of gold
No need to be cold
No need to be cold

I understand
I will ask nicely to not
Stay - alone.

O.A.

**Love in a Covid-19 Era**

Do you mind if I call you?
From a distance -
Safe social distance
Or hug you from a few meters away
I know we're lightyears apart
Like the Earth, Sun and Moon
Orbiting each other like cosmic debris
But believe me
I long for the day
When we can hold each other
In a closer way
Love in a Covid-19 Era
Love in a Covid-19 Era
There's so much more I could say
But believe me
I long for the day
When we can talk to each other
In a closer way.

O.A.

## Ode to the Paramedics

I once wanted to be one
But it takes a certain person
To be a hero everyday
And this is not me
Unfortunately.
However,
I tip my hat off to you
For the things that you do
From starting an I.V.
To chest compressions
To pain management therapy
Everytime I see you, on the road
I am reminded I once needed help
And you were there to save me from
The cold...

I tip my hat off to you
For the things that you do.
Thank you.

O.A.

## Forsaken

I have been forsaken
Left out to dry
On an island of time
Hourglass of tumultuous time
Hourglass of tumultuous time
Forlorned and grief-stricken
Only to wade in rising waters
Rising waters

There was a ship
That passed by the island
But I distantly shelved all notions
Of boarding the vessel...
Of boarding the vessel...

Forsaken Not Forgotten
Forsaken Not Forgotten
The ship will leave me
The crew and members will bereave
However, as I sip coconut water
And swim with the salty fish
I will wonder
Did I do the right thing?
By not mingling?
By not mingling?

An hourglass
Of tumultuous time.

O.A.

## If I Say Goodbye

If I walk out that door
And say goodbye
Will you break down
And cry?

If I say I'm leaving
With the sunset
Will you be sad
And have regrets?

If I tell you that I loved you all my life
Will you believe me
And change your mind
And save me?

If I walk out that door
And say goodbye
Will you break down
And cry?

If I walk out that door
And say goodbye
Will you break down
And cry?

O.A.

## To the Red Baron

Sorry old friend
That I have not written to you
After university
We promised to stay in touch.
To be quite honest
I miss you dearly with your camera
So very very much.

I still have your letters
That you wrote me
But I haven't had time
Because I've been fighting for my life
With all the wolves outside my door...
Yes, I know it's sad.

I hope you're well
And still writing...
As you can see
I'm still trying
To be me
And be free...
Good day old friend.

O.A.

## Of Theme & Variation

In the exposition
Of theme & variation
Of allegory & pain
Of a world uneasy
Of a world trying to be

There was tempo
Vivo non rubato
There was fortissimo
Vivo non rubato
And there was legato
Vivo non rubato

In the composition
Of theme & variation
Of humans creating
Of a piece enthralling
Of a piece temptating

There were dynamics
Fire and ice
There were rules
Fire and ice
There were regulations
Fire and ice

In the coda
Of theme & variation
Of the beginning of the end
Of a beautiful composition
Of a piece without competition

There are people listening
An audience
There are people believing
An audience
There are people humming
An audience

Of musical appreciation
Of classical & jazz notation
Of the roots & stems

Of augmenting stipulations
Of a I-V-I cadence
In theme & variation

In theme & variation
In theme & variation
In theme & variation
In theme & variation
Of a world
Forever changing
Of a world
Forever changing

O.A.

## Humble Pie

Dear Oliver,
You have it twisted
You cannot write
So what's the use in trying?
Round and round
They go
Circling in a merry-go round
Circling in a merry-go round
Around in my head;
Around in my head;
But if you're lucky
Someone might read you
Once you're finally dead...
Time is not on your side
Except in the timecapsule
You buried...
Where you keep
Hope alive...

O.A.

## The Ethereal Kingdom

On an opaque ceiling of clouds
On a stretch of mile long skytowns
There was an ethereal kingdom
The kingdom of heaven
The palace in which he lived;
And in this kingdom,
Angels, cherubims, seraphims
And celestial beings resided.
It was spectral and cozy
Up on the clouds of skytown,
Until one day a spirit named Lemures
Wanted to journey back down,
Down to earth again.
He told God that he was lost
Without the woman he loved
He had been in a car accident
But she was still living on
So as fair as God was
He gave Lemures 3 tasks
To complete before dawn...

1. Lemures had to battle a sphinx
On the other side of heaven
2. He had to fly to the moon
And paint a face on it's surface
3. He had to promise, if he found her
He would bring her back from earth
And live out the rest of his days
Unperturbed and undisturbed, with her.

These 3 things he would do
To be with his widowed wife soon.
Lemures figured he could battle a sphinx
And bring her back from earth too
But he did not know, how he would
Fly to the moon?
The 1st task was simple enough
On the other side of heaven
Lived the gatekeeper
Between time and space,
A sphinx with a stoic and weathered face.
Lemures took a halo and trident spear

And flew to see it there...

When he arrived,
He looked it in it's eyes
And told him why he came tonight
All this way about his wife
And God's challenge here
But without further incident
The sphinx felt sorry for him
And speared himself with the trident...
With the battle won
The gate into time and space was open
So Lemures began his journey
To the moon, to paint a face of someone,
Someone he once loved.
Through time and space
Through the void of darkness
Through the infinite starlight
Lemures flew nearing the moon
Once he got there, he picked a spot
Then used the halo he got
And sprinkled pixie dust
All around the place, until he drew a face
With a heart around the shape.
So with these 2 feats complete
Lemure flew back to heaven
The Ethereal Kingdom
And told God about his 2 conquests
And stated he only had 1 more left.

Without further ado,
God wished him luck
After looking up at the face in the moon
And told him never to give up
After all he'd been through
And with this bid him adieu
Sending him back to earth
To look for his widowed wife "Sue."
At his request, Lemures
Travelled back down to earth
To be with his wife in turn
And found out, when he got there
He had been burned
Because she was not in Vancouver

Anymore.
She had died a few days before.

Sue was in Hell,
Taken down by Beezlebub
And some archangels
Because she had swallowed some pills.
Lemures was beside himself.

So he spread his wings
And counted his blessings
And made the dark journey
Into Pandemonium.
In the shadow of the valley of death
The city of gold
Lemures searched for Sue
And found her alone
All alone
In a sanctimonious cathedral.
"Sue?" he spoke, "I've come to get you...
To bring you back...
To bring you back...
To bring you back..."

The stark words
Echoed throughout eternity...
Lemures gathered himself
And put his head on Sue's chest
"If we give up now, he's won...
Can I sing to you like I used to my love?"
Sue's eyes were cold.
"Here is a lullaby, you used to know
That we used to sing, back home...

Can I sing you a song
About the world gone wrong
Will you get upset
And move me along?
If I belt out a tune
About myself and you
Will you get furious
And start singing the blues?"

Sue's eyes started to open brighter

She then turned to face Lemures
The words came out shakey
But definitely brighter:

"I only want to sing
You a fantastic lullaby
About the future of the world
And the cloud city in the sky!
I only want to sing
You a fantastic lullaby
About the future of the world
And the heaven I like..."

Sue quietly sang the words
To the lullaby in her husband's face
Lemures immediately held her
Deep into his strong embrace.
The 2 left the cathedral
And began their journey
Leaving the city of gold
Leaving Pandemonium;
And as the 2 soulmates
Flew higher and higher
On Lemures ethereal wings
The city of gold
Began to crumble
Dismantle turning into rubble.
There were earthquakes
Lightning and thunder...
There were earthquakes
Lightning and thunder...

Once the 2 soulmates
Arrived back in heaven
The celebrations began:
Angels, cherubims and seraphims
All gathered around
Lemures and Sue...
To hear the story
Of what they had been through...
The festivities carried on
Into the night
And when daylight
Daylight came:

God asked Lemures, "what would they do?"
Lemures turned to Sue and said:
"Now that I have you
There's nothing we cannot do
My love for you is real
If you look up, I even painted your face
In the moon..."
Sue looked up and cried.

They lived forever together
In heaven, for the rest
Rest of their celestial lives
Under God's watchful eyes
In the Ethereal Kingdom...

O.A.

## T.U.T.S. in the Summer

My friend, the Piano Man and I
Used to attend
Theater Under the Stars
With all our friends
In the summers of high school.

To watch a musical:
Like Grease
Or Miss Saigon
Or Sunday in the Park with George
Or West Side Story
On sunny nights or rainy days
In Stanley Park, was alot of fun.
I learned alot about the stage
Volunteering to turn the page
For violinists in the pit orchestra.

If you brought a blanket
And some bug spray
And loved the musical display -
In the summers of my childhood
It was a good way to spend the day.

O.A.

## Frontline Workers

There's no need for you to work
Yet you do because of your own reasons
And it's because you do
That our economy
Is sustaining through
You are a blessed soul
My hero through the rain and snow
Because you do what I cannot do
Risk your life to help others
And yet you tell me it's no bother
And I see this and know
Karma will help you grow
When you least expect it
Your working hands are a blessing
And I won't ever forget it -
I won't ever forget it.
Thank you.

O.A.

## DreamLife

Like an ad from Total Recall
I want to live my best life
Inside a machine
Inside a VR world
I want to be the best version of me
And only feel good
And only see the truth
Live your best life
Live like everything is right
Live like there's only one day -
DreamLife.

I want to put on a suit
With sensors, and gloves
No controllers
Inside a machine
Inside a VR world
I want to be the best version of me
And be who I want to be
And that means anybody
Live your best life
Live like everything is right
Live like there's only one day -
DreamLife.

A Dungeons and Dragons RPG
Or Sci-fi FPS
A world where I can roam free
A mapped out oddessy
Inside a machine
Inside a VR world
I want to be the best version of me
And be who I want to be
And that means anybody
Live your best life
Live like everything is right
Live like there's only one day -
DreamLife.

I'll pay the pretty price
Of the cost of a suit that has lights
No matter how expensive

Because I want to escape this life
And have a Virtual Reality Avatar
And so I can travel anywhere and far

Use the VR world for work
Simulate training for employees first
A world where I can train me
A mapped out oddessy
Inside a machine
Inside a VR world
I want to be the best version of me
And be who I want to be
And that means anybody
Live your best life
Live like everything is right
Live like there's only one day -
DreamLife.

O.A.

## Cascading Tides of the Moon

I used to be afraid
To get shipwrecked on a beach
To get flooded out at sea
But then the power
Of the waning moon
Saved me

She was my saviour
She was my beautiful muse
Inspiring me with every orbiting turn
Her inspiration was ever so daunting
And she came to me
As a cascading source of beauty
Changing the tides of my life
Chasing out the dark and bringing light
Making the waves wash me back out to sea
Making the waves wash me back out to sea

The power of the moon
Is more than you can believe
If she loves you, you'll be free
To float about the everchanging sea
The everchanging sea

And she came to me
As a cascading source of beauty
Changing the tides of my life
Chasing out the dark and bringing light
Making the waves wash me back out to sea
Making the waves wash me back out to sea

The power of the moon
Is more than you can believe
If she loves you, you'll be free
You'll be free
You'll be free

O.A.

## All That I Am

I'm a simple man
I don't need much
I like good music
I like good food
All that I am
Is a simple man

All that I am
Is a drifter without a plan
Not a very smart dude
But I like good music
And I like good food
All that I am
Is a simple man

I got a big heart
I cry in certain parts
Insecure most of the time
I love words
And their etymology in rhymes
All that I am
Is a simple man

Some may call me old
Or old fashioned
But I don't mind
I like good music
I like good food
I love to Dance
I do love to Dance
But honestly,

All that I am
Is a simple man.

O.A.

## Macabre Silhouettes

Daunting apparitions
Haunting all that I see
I don't expect anyone
To save me from me
To save me from me
Shadows of everyone
That got the best of me
Me, me, me...

Macabre silhouettes
On my walls in my mind
It's what I feel inside
I don't expect anyone
To save me from me
To save me from me
Shadows of everyone
That got the best of me
Me, me, me...

I don't expect anyone
To save me from me
To save me from me
Shadows of everyone
That got the best of me
Me, me, me...

I don't expect anyone
To save me from me
To save me from me
Shadows of everyone
That got the best of me
Me, me, me...

O.A.

## 21

The house always wins
Blackjack never loved me
They said I wasn't black enough...
They said the same thing
About Alexander Dumas
Although, I do not think I am
Alexander Dumas...

How do you love me?
Let me count the ways
If I starve will you laugh
And serve me humble pie?

The house always wins
We know this, yes we do, we
But its God's house
Let me live
Let me live
Past the dealer's hands
I don't want to lose the game
To a man or woman
Who smokes crack on his breaks

The house always wins
21 Blackjack
I will walk away from the table of life
Let me live
Let me live
I will walk away from the dealer's hands
Bloodstained
From winning too much
Let me live
Let me live
Please.

I won't show you my cards
If you don't show me yours
That way we both win.

O.A.

## Handpicked by Me

If I love you unconditionally
Without reservations
Will you love me back
For this dissertation?
I only want to see you
Succeed in all areas of life -
But you think I want to undermine you
And backstab you with a knife
Mom I love you, believe me
But you are blind to our unity
I only want to help you
But you seem to feel overdue
Like a book from the library
Unread, unappreciated and blue
But that's not true
That's not true
I see you and feel your pain
Believe me, when I say -

"I love you."

O.A.

## Reveal Yourself

I have had a hard time
Trying to better myself
But instead I've acquired poor health
Now and forever
I need my true self
To appear

In the mirror I look for him
But he is hiding
In my reflection
In my shadow
I only want to be better
Than myself
The self I know
So I say to myself:
The self must grow -

Water my garden of truth
Let it sprout beautiful vegetation
Let it bloom with each morning
Let me grow God from the self
The self that I run from and know
Like the mirror I stare into with sorrow
Like the mirror I stare into with sorrow
Let me be translucent -
Let me say:
Reveal Yourself!

And the madman go...

O.A.

## English Bay

To watch the fireworks
Each year that I have
To watch the different countries
Compete for the chance
To be victorious
In having the best fireworks display
The brightest colours
In all of English Bay
Is something special
That most people cherish
To this very day.
To meet with friends
Sit on the beach 'till the end
On a blanket looking up in the sky
Allows people to absorb the lights
The shapes, colours and drones' flights.

The way in which this fusion aligns
Most countries that participate each time
Is a perfect display of the multicultured way
Vancouver B.C. shows off it's true colours
Every year to this very day...

O.A.

## Hold On a Little Longer

I know you're anxious
Feel like jumping out of your skin
Weight of the world is great
Don't feel like yourself
Anymore
Anymore

But trust me when I say
Hold on a little longer
Stay awhile
Put down your coat
Put away your shoes
Hold on a little longer
If you got the blues

I see past your smile
Broken more than one time
Weight of the world is great
Don't feel like yourself
Anymore
Anymore

But trust me when I say
Hold on a little longer
Stay awhile
Put down your coat
Put away your shoes
Hold on a little longer
If you got the blues

Hold on a little longer
Stay awhile
Put down your coat
Put away your shoes
Hold on a little longer
If you got the blues

Don't do what you want to
Think it through
I got you
I got you

O.A.

## Lightyears Away

On the horizon
Lightyears away
Lost out at sea
Is someone for me
Is someone for me
In a ship of destiny
Destiny
Maybe she'll hear me
Calling out to her
Maybe she won't see
Me waving a flag
Waving a white flag
Surrendering
Surrendering to her
As she drifts on by
And I kneel to the sky
And ask God why?
I will wait on the shore
Until she circles by
Around the Earth
On the sea once more
For my muse forlorned
Forlorned
Lost out at sea
Is someone for me
Is someone for me
In a ship of destiny
Destiny

O.A.

## The Gravity of the Situation

If you'll come with me
I want to learn to fly safely
You don't need to hold my hands
But I want you to be there to see
That I can be someone who flies free
When I spread my wings like Icarus
And fly by the sun, only I won't be done
And I'll try to write home as often as I can
Unless I'm caught up in some place
Far far away

If you'll come with me
I want to learn to fly safely
You don't need to hold my hands
But I want you to understand
My wings won't melt if I'm by myself
When I spread my wings like Icarus
And fly by the sun, only I won't be done
And I'll try to write home as often as I can
Unless I'm caught up in some place
Far far away

I need to loosen the gravity
Surrounding me and learn to fly
Far far away

O.A.

## Arts and Letters

There they go:
A Person
Of Arts and Letters
With a book on their mind
With letters to sign
Trying to get published
Trying to vault the stratosphere
Trying to undermine the fear
Trying to walk the walk
And write the write here;
Trying to seek the truth
And offer another route,
One less travelled through.

There they go:
A Person
Of Arts and Letters
Trying to move heaven and earth
Once again
Trying to put the devil in his place
Once again
Or unleash the hounds to no end
Like all those before them
Like all those before them
With simply, a sharp mind and words -
Just words.

O.A.

## The Fortress On Morally High Ground

In my mind,
A thousand men want to stab me with their pens
A thousand Samuri want to end my poetic defense
I am no Philosopher, no Prophet, just a mere Poet
Trying to know right from wrong
Trying to write my best song
In a world that has no more room for us
The people who think outloud but must
Think outloud must

In my mind,
I journey to the Fortress on morally high ground
To see him, the one everyone loves around
He is wise, far beyond me
I'm just a poetic belligerent idiot, you see
Trying to save his world from falling down
Trying to save face from a fallen disgrace
That I've become
That I've become

In my own defense of poetry,
The world needs more light
So if you have the need to shine
Speak your mind,
Ideas are worth more than ever
In this Information World
And walk the line
Everytime
Everytime
Poetry still has value
In the Fortress in my mind...
In the Fortress in my mind...

O.A.

## To #24, Forevermore

I hope no one minds
If I say a few words
To recognize
One of the top 3
Basketball players
Of all time...
This is a tribute
To a great man
Who understood
The hardwood
And lived up
To God's plan...

Poised, ready to strike -
The Black Mamba
Shakes and bakes
And doesn't hesitate
With the ball in his hands
He executes a turn
Around jump shot
With the clock at 5 seconds
The crowd cheers and they beckon
For him to do it all over again
Cheering and chanting
His name... Kobe! Kobe! Kobe!
Black Mamba strikes again
And again, and again
Leaving his opponents breathless
Leaving his opponents breathless
Leaving his opponents breathless.

20 seasons with the Lakers
Multiple MVPs and accolades
But still he was on a quest
To leave a legacy and be great
When he retired
He went on a farewell tour
And was rewired
Unlike any great player before
In saying farewell
To every fan, in every arena
Up close and personal

And even though it must of been hard
No one could tell
No one could tell
No one could tell.

"Dear Basketball"
Said how everyone felt
About the player inside them
And captured the hearts
Of both women and men
"Dear Basketball"
Was a great poem
And moment for the ages
He stood taller than tall
On the world's stages
Number 24?
No one could ask you
For anything more...
Number 24?
I hope
You're still soaring
Through the sands of time
Through the halls of greatness
Through heaven's courts
Wherever you are...
Wherever you are...
You are legend
You are folklore
You will be missed
But not forgotten:
Forevermore
Forevermore
Forevermore.

O.A.

## Way, Way Too Short

Lives cut way, way too short
Longing for them
To come back through the door
Waiting up all night
Waiting until sunlight
Waiting 'till morning dawns
But we know it's a lost cause.

Lives cut way, way too short
Longing for them
To come back through the door
Wanting the best outcome
Wanting the moon and sun
Wanting 'till tears are done
But we know it's a lost cause.

Lives cut way, way too short
Gone too soon
And wanting them
All of them
To come back through the door

Lives cut way, way too short
Gone too soon
And wanting them
All of them
To come back through the door

Only time can allow
Only time can allow
Only time can allow
Our loved ones
To come back down
To come back down
To come back down
We've done all we can
We've done all we can
We've done all we can
It's up to God now.

O.A.

## It's Hard to Believe

These days
It's hard to believe
You're still with me
You're still with me

I thought you would have left
A long time ago, out the window
As a little bird looking for something
I thought you would have left me
In this brittle day and age of suffering

But you're still here
It's hard to believe
You're still with me
You're still with me

And I still believe in you
My faith
My compass
My refuge

It's hard to believe
You're still with me
You're still with me

These days.

O.A.

## Transcendental

Imagine a world without pain
A world with nothing for gain
A trancendental world
Between time and space
And the only way to live
In this realm
Was to balance the scales
On a metaphysical pendulum.
The only way to live
Was to allow for more freedom
Was to allow for more freedom
Between folks and their friends
In this transcendental, magical,
Exceptional, prolific, conceptual,
Intercontinental, transcendental,
Realm...

Imagine this world
And you will begin
To understand
Heaven.

O.A.

## NeoWise The Luminous Comet

Streaking across an ephemeral sky
As a golden ball of fire tonight
I see a gaseous orb of radiant light
Brighter and brighter burning bright
Coming down through earth's skyline.
The last time I watched a falling star
Burn up, was Hailey's Comet years ago;
But oh how NeoWise shines so bright
I wish I could see it for one more night
Before it becomes a dusty earthstone
Crashing to the ground,
Never to be found,
At daylight.

O.A.

## The Sword Shaped Moon

My heart is on fire
When I see the moon
Sword shaped and higher
Than it was the night before
How I wish you could see it too!

O.A.

## If I Had a Chance to Record Again

If I had a chance to record music again
I would not try to sing,
Or play outside my comfort zone.
I would record without out words
Downtempo, electric or new age jazz
Retrograde beats to listen to again
Or just some classical records
With my cello or violin
This is where my head is
Trying to figure out what I like the best.
My Red Ocean album my friends
Is what I would try to duplicate
If I had the chance to record again...
If I had the chance to record again...

O.A.

## These are Not Great Pieces

These are not great pieces of literature
But rather quips and quivers
Of presumptuous anecdotes
Of songs of tribute
Of precocious matters
Of things I revell in
In times of wonder and delight

If you would like to see great pieces:
Check Langston Hughes
Amy Lowell
Leonard Cohen
Phyllis Webb
Margaret Atwood
Sylvia Plath
Lorna Crozier
Walt Whitman
T.S. Eliot
Maya Angelou
Sharon Thesen
Rudyard Kipling
Among many others for great examples.

I only wish to pass the time
Forging words and rhymes
That I can turn to later and exclaim:
I wrote a poem that is mine!
During Covid-1-9.

O.A.

## My Violin

My violin sings
When I play its strings
In a prelude or concerto
By Handel, Correlli or Paganini
Or by any composer who is dear to me.

If I rossin its bow
It will take me anywhere I want to go
As I ferociously play the strings staccato;
But to make it firm and tighten the hold
I only need to pluck it fiercely with bravado.

If I play it gently
It will let me know it is appreciated
As I beautifully play the strings legato;
But it only sings if I pull and push slowly
I only need to bow it lovingly with bravado.

Yes, my violin
Like me enjoys the pulling of its strings
But the conversation turns
When I bow in reverse
And let it all go
Rubato.

My violin
And I
Have a history.

O.A.

## Symphony of Regrets

Swirling in my head
In a whirlpool of thoughts
Like shards of broken glass
Scattered across a hot floor
Are a thousand cut up feet
Trying to walk across the Danube River
Escaping their homeland
Of broken dreams -
What I tell myself
In solitude
Is to walk hard
Walk fast, through the ruins
Of what was, and what is to come
And do not mind the symphony of music
Plagal, dissonant and cadenced
Of regretable decisions
That a thousand feet have made
That a thousand feet have made
In trying to bear fruit
To their trancendiant dreams.

The Roman Ruins we all see
In our minds
Are centuries of people
Building up
And tearing down
What they believe.

O.A.

## Opinions, Thoughts, Ideas and Words

A train of thought
Is an opinion
Or a string of ideas
Formulated into words.

A word is an idea
Or thought that forms
An expressed opinion
Between a thought and idea.

A thought has both
A positive and negative charge
An idea is always positive
Because it brings change
As a word; singular word
Or expressed opinion.

Once a thought is conjured up
It becomes an idea
By assigning words to it
Which was a thought.

But originally
What comes first
Is the thought
Because it requires
A picture, taste, touch
Smell or sound
To be associated with it...

Which to you comes first?
Opinions, thoughts, ideas or words?

O.A.

# For the Love of Nature and Machines

There's a place I know
Far away from my humble abode
A far cry from my quiet and quaint home
A castle on a sandy deserted beach
A church steeple no one can reach
A central safe haven for only me
Where I go when I want to be alone
And it suffocates me to know you want me
Want me to give up the world I believe
The world that I created within me
Just so you can grow your company
Just so you can slow down empathy
And turn a profit
Turn a profit

There's a place I know
Far away from the avatars of home
A place where lush greenery still grows
A place where animals can still roam
A place where water creatures can live
A habitat in the deep temperate wilderness
Where I go when I want to be alone
And it suffocates me to know you want me
Want me to give up the world I believe
The world that I created within me
Just so you can grow your company
Just so you can slow down empathy
And turn a profit
Turn a profit

Evolution exists
Evolution exists
But mitigation persists
To be cold hearted
When ordinary people resist
When ordinary people resist

A natural habitat
Is all that and more for wildlife
Is all that when changes mean strife
The world is blue and green
The world is blue and green

The world is love and machines
The world is love and machines
The world is changing drastically
The world is changing drastically

Evolution exists
Evolution exists
But mitigation persists
To be cold hearted
When ordinary people resist
When ordinary people resist

Love and machines
Love and machines
Let's let love change our means
Let's let love augment our dreams

Love and machines
Love and machines
Let's let love change our means
Let's let love augment our dreams

Let's let the machines
Rule with love
And love rule the machines.

O.A.

## The Bridge from Here to Eternity

Tighten your lips
Clench your fists
Tighten your steps
You're a wreck
You're a wreck
The accident was real
The other car hit you
Did you feel? Do you feel?

Step outside your body
Step in front of everyone
Step outside your body
Flesh meets your blood
Step outside your body
Step into the lucid sun
Step across the bridge
From here to eternity

From here to eternity
There is a bridge to cross
Walk the skyline
Walk across, walk across
Meet your lifeline
See your timeline
Unfold as you bear it all
Unfold as you bear it all

Step outside your body
Step in front of everyone
Step outside your body
Flesh meets your blood
Step outside your body
Step into the lucid sun
Step across the bridge
From here to eternity

Tighten your lips
Clench your fists
Tighten your steps
You're a wreck
You're a wreck
The accident was real

The other car hit you
Did you feel? Do you feel?

From here to eternity
There is a bridge to cross
Walk the skyline
Walk across, walk across
Meet your lifeline
See your timeline
Unfold as you bear it all
Unfold as you bear it all

Walk the skyline
Walk across, walk across.

O.A.

## P.S. Paginated Sequence

In the top level drawer
And in my closet too
Of my room
Before I left it
You'll find
All the letters
I wrote you
Citing how
Vile, and incomprehensible
You were to me
And how
I longed
For the day
When I could tell you
This dirty little secret:
"I owe you money..."

O.A.

## Mr. Archer's Theme

This is Mr. Archer's theme
He's the richest man
I've ever seen.
Pretentious as hell
But I love how his Rolex
And Raybans gleam!

He started out with 5 bucks
When he was 17
And traded the 5 bucks
For a blender for good luck.
Then he made lemonade
Out of blended lemons
And sold the juice for 25 cents
Until he made 245 dollars
In loose change.
Then when he was 19
He was hired to change tires
At Canadian Tire
Where he went to nightschool
And became a manager there too.
Finally, after all his sweat and tears
He ended up owning a dealership
By the time he was 30
He was hungry and thirsty
For success.
But I digress;
I met Mr. Archer once
When I was looking for a car
He told me to be patient
Stay focused and I would go far.
Although he was wrong
I can't help but praise his song:

This is Mr. Archer's theme
He's the richest man
I've ever seen.
Pretentious as hell
But I love how his Rolex
And Raybans gleam!

Maybe being pretentious helps?

I dunno but I love how his Rolex
And Raybans gleam!

O.A.

## O, How Time Flies!

Yesterday I was playing basketball
As a 20 year old man
In my beloved City of Coquitlam
Now I'm an older man
Grown up in a new system
Grown up in a new system
Through the winter, summer, fall
I recall a desire to write down it all
But in the cusp of every spring
I would loosen my grip on everything
And celebrate the important things
In my life, every year, with every mile
The present is forever crashing piles
Into tomorrow's desktop of program files
But that makes life, so worthwhile
But that makes life, so worthwhile
The beauty of the work of the beguiled
O, how time flies!
How time flies!

O.A.

## Deer Lake Park

If you've ever watched a show
In Deer Lake Park
You will know it's a magical place
For the acoustics
Open to the air
Great for summer fairs
It's one of the best places to watch
The VSO, just so you know.

Pull up a lawn chair
And stay awhile...
Listen to the sounds
Of a summer festival now
Or visit the museum grounds
Behind the grassy mounds.

There's a boardwalk around the place
That I love to take, a walkway
That brings you around Burnaby lake
And like I said, if you're with friends
It's a great place to catch a show,
Anytime you go.

O.A.

## Great Expectations

This was my favorite book growing up
Because the fisherman who gave up
On life was given one last chance
To make something of his life
Thanks to a benefactor he helped...
The story was about Karma
And the resilience of the human spirit
And there was dancing
Lots of dancing...
Unfortunately, as I've learned
Books like this are for dreamers
And happy endings don't belong in life
But only in the books and movies
Now we have great expectations
Living in a Covid-19 world
Living in a Covid-19 world
Testing the resilience
Of the human spirit
Testing

O.A.

## Admired for Awhile

I've always marvelled
At how Lord Byron earned money
For his poetry and Keats
Struggled to survive...
It would be nice to earn money
For the simple rhymes
I have Authorized
But in fact, to even be thought of,
In times of coffee and tea
Admirable reflection
Without being told
Is enough to keep me bold
To keep writing 'till I'm old...

O.A.

## Train Like No Tomorrow

As a new day dawns
And the world is moving on
Carpe diem
Carpe diem
He wants this:
12 rounds with the champ
25 minutes in the octagon
But he's not convinced
He's not convinced
That he can win!
So he puts his head down
And says a prayer
Carpe diem
Carpe diem
Will he be there?
Train like no tomorrow
Train like no tomorrow
Train like no one else cares

He wants him
In his corner
To be with his cutman
To be the stones in his hands
To be the cinderblocks in demand
Like Cinderella Man
In case this time
He was out of his mind
Challenging the champ
Challenging the champ
Dancing with the devil
Dancing with the devil
In a prickly round, dance.
Carpe diem
Carpe diem
A fight for the ages
A fight for prize wages
A fight to beat the odds
This full contact fighter
Is the underdog
But it doesn't matter to him
Because he is good
A good fighter

Against the odds.
A good fighter
Against the odds.

O.A.

## Love

Love is a ring of fire
Love is walking a highwire
Love is scaling the highest walls
Love is a castle that will not fall
Love is a war between enemies
Love is a scar that will heal indefinitely
Love is the greatest thing on Earth
Love is the best source of light unfurled
Love is the greatest thing

But when Love is reversed
It is the darkest source of evoL

Evol is a way to hate someone
Evol is the dark side of the sun
Evol is the world not giving a damn
Evol is the war that lovers misunderstand
Evol is a two-sided or two-faced person
Evol is a different kind of light beacon
Evol is the worse thing on Earth
Evol is a mirror that has broken
Evol is the worse thing

Love can be Evol
Evol can be Love
Love...

O.A.

## My Favorite Black Hat

I've had the pleasure
Of wearing alot of hats over the years
But my favorite one
That I absolutely love to wear
Is my black Michael Jordan
Flight symbol- Mercedes Benz -
Baseball Cap.

I've had Beanies, Berets, Bucket Hats
And Fedoras; even liked to wear
A Paperboy Kango
At one time long ago

But you know what?
My favorite black hat
Has never had me looking bad
Or looking back
In the mirror
So I will rock it
'Till it falls apart
And it's inferior...

O.A.

## To Harry Jerome

The title of 'Fastest Man on Earth'
Belonged to you Mr. Harry Jerome
At one or a few points
In your track and field career.
You set 7 track records
In your time here
And on the track
You were heavily feared.
As a 100 meter sprint fan
I must admit 10 seconds
Was pretty fast
And your record last until
You broke it again with 9.4 in 1964.

Once more
I am most proud
That you were Canadian
And represented Canada
Throughout your career
On a world stage
Again and again
And were heavily revered
'Till the very end.

O.A.

## Piper's Lagoon

As a young boy I came here
Swimming in the ocean
Running through forest trails
And spending time at Piper's.
The Lagoon was where
I learned Wado Ryu
In the open fields of grass
In my Sensei's class
On Friday nights too.
Sometimes I would run down
The trail into the secret cove
And spend time with friends
Fishing, in the Lagoon trough;
And sometimes I would swim
With the Jellyfish in the ocean
And get stung on my feet
And laugh in the open...

Such great memories
I have with you
Since we've spoken
Of Piper's Lagoon.

O.A.

## Mythopoeia

The shadow of a man
Is always larger than he stands
It tells a Tall Tale better than he can
But only his friends will understand
How a silhouette can be cast
How a silhouette can be cast
Against the burning sun.

Mythopoeia
Myth and the poem
Myth and the poesis
Mythopoeia
Madness and utopia
Madness and utopia
Mythopoeia

The story of a Unicorn
Is made from everyone else
It's not real unless it's believable in itself
But the myth goes on and on
Unless facts are gone
Unless facts are gone
To make a short story long.

Mythopoeia
Myth and the poem
Myth and the poesis
Mythopoeia
Madness and utopia
Madness and utopia
Mythopoeia

Mythopoeia
Myth and the poem
Myth and the poesis
Mythopoeia
Madness and utopia
Madness and utopia
Mythopoeia

O.A.

## The True Sparrow

In my backyard
There is a plum tree
Singular as can be
One day a true sparrow
Came to me
And sat firmly nested
In that ripe tree.
Grey billed, and browned
This eurasian bird
Sat back and watched me
As I raked up leaves.
As I raked up leaves.

Here in B.C.
Sparrows have a common
Tendency to occupy
All types of lives
In their natural habitats...
But spiritually
Seeing a sparrow
Offers a sense of responsibility
And community
So I thought I should continue
Raking up the leaves
Around where it left the tree;

Before it took off
With a purple plum
With a purple plum
Purple plum
And forlorned me...

O.A.

## Digital Rain

Computer syntax
Clouds my screen
Falling bits and bytes
Down on my programs
As digital rain showers light
On the matrix of my nightlife.
10110110001010101010010

O.A.

## Singularity of the Rose

Eyes, wide open
Eyes, to be broken
I only want to cross over
And not be spoken
Of as someone who's woken

It's getting late now
And the show is almost done
It's getting late now
And victory is among us
And victory is among us
Who will lament the broken one?

Eyes, wide open
Eyes, to be broken
I only want to cross over
And not be spoken
Of as someone who's woken

It's getting late now
And the show is almost done
It's getting late now
And victory is among us
And victory is among us
Who will lament the broken one?

Time constraints
Time will not wait
Time for another time
Time for another rhyme

Eyes, wide open
Eyes, to be broken
I only want to cross over
And not be spoken
Of as someone who's woken

Outside in the cold
Outside the box of stone
Outside the gates
Inside I should wait!

Eyes, wide open
Eyes, to be broken
I only want to cross over
And not be spoken
Of as someone who's woken

Holding the metal rose
Holding the metal rose
Turning inwardly
Round and round
Round and round
As a petal falls and flows

Eyes, wide open
Eyes, to be broken
I only want to cross over
And not be spoken
Of as someone who's woken

Holding the metal rose
Holding the metal rose
Turning inwardly
Round and round
Round and round
As a petal falls and flows

Eyes, wide open
Eyes, to be broken
I only want to cross over
And not be spoken
Of as someone who's woken

Falling in the garden
Falling in the garden
Falling in the garden
Of flowers

Lavender blue
I see you
Lavender blue
I see you

Falling in the garden
Falling in the garden

Falling in the garden
Of flowers

Lavender blue
I see you
Lavender blue
I see you

But this rose
The petals fall
The petals flow

A thorn or two
Lavender blue
I see you
I see you

I am woke
Since we last
Spoke.

A thorn or two
Lavender blue
I see you
I see you

O.A.

## Celebration

It's a celebration
It's a revelation
Of your life
Of your hard times
Of who you were
And who you became
Raise a glass
Make a toast
For your success
For your happiness
That you achieved in life.

It's a celebration
It's a revelation
Of your life
I will not forget you
I will remember you
And your synergy
Never forget your energy
You will be missed
You will be laid to rest
With the rest of your family.

It's a celebration
It's a revelation
Of your life
Of your time on Earth
Of your hard work
And I hope you see this
And know you're missed
Sorely missed
As someone who left us -
Someone who was infectious -
Too soon you were filled with love.
LOVE.

O.A.

## Sitting on a Bench in Granville Island

In sitting on a bench
In Granville Island
Feeding the pigeons
And insatiable seagulls
I find myself enjoying
The fresh clean air.

The market is near by
So I might pick up
Something for dinner.
But before I leave
I might catch a show
At the Arts Club Theater
Or visit some of the shops
Before I go...

In sitting on a bench
In Granville Island
Feeding the pigeons
And insatiable seagulls
I'm reminded how beautiful
The scenery here is -
And why it's a pleasure to know.
One of Vancouver's
Many -
Treasure troves...

O.A.

**The Voice Within**

Darkness hides
A spark of wuthering light
Incandescent and perpetually bright
Deep in the recesses of everyone inside
And it's a tribulation to fighting hard times.

And it comes from a place of strength
It is a blessing to find it heaven sent
Your own inner voice as it bends
Propells it's way up from your diaphram
It is a choice you make to use it's magic.

The voice within will always win
Because it's prowess is beautiful
Because it's struggle is real
The outer voice can't compete
With the inner sensation of how you feel
And that's the real deal.

The voice within will always win
Because it's prowess is beautiful
Because it's struggle is real
The outer voice can't compete
With the inner sensation of how you feel
And that's the real deal.

O.A.

## The Counterpoint of Love

I love you
Don't you see
It's me for you
And you for me
We are poets          I love you
The poet and poetes  Don't you see
You are the best      It's me for you
You are my best friend And you for me
                     We are poets
                     The poet and poetes

You are the best
You are my best friend
                     We are poets
                     The poet and poetes


Refrain:
Don't you see
It's me for you
And you for me       We are poets
                     The poet and poetes


The impetus
Is inside our world:
The poem.
                     We are poets
                     The poet and poetes


O.A.

## Enamoured by You

I don't mean to put you
On a pedastal
But in my mind
That's where you belong
Like a Picasso painting
You hang on the wall of my eyes
Will you be inspiring me
Like the beautiful Eiffel Tower?
Or will you be leaving me
On the first plane out of Paris?
I only want you to stay
And talk for awhile...
You hang on the wall of my eyes
As a picture perfect portrait
That I would like to see again
Another time...

O.A.

# The Legend of the Grey Wolf and Brown Beaver

A Purely Fictitious Canadian Ballad:
Told to me by my Grandfather before he died...

In the deepest part of the temperate forest
Near the mouth of the Chilko River
There was a lodging dam of a little fellow
It belonged to a friendly Brown Beaver

It was a rainy, damp, dismal day
And the Brown Beaver's lodging had caved
In the wind and strong showering rain
He needed a few logs to be replaced

He had seen a few pieces of loose timber
Up at the mouth of the Chilko River
So he decided to journey to the spot
Where he last saw the forest logs

The Brown Beaver needed to fix it soon
Before the end and it was around noon
There were holes in his lodging
That were exposed on his lodging roof

But just last month a friend of his died
A furry mouse that loved his water house
It has gotten eaten by a sea otter
On its way out, out by the river mouth

So on his journey upriver to the mouth
The Brown Beaver was watching out
For any sea otters that came around
Looking to cause trouble on his grounds

And when it finally arrived
To gather a few logs on the side
It carried them in it's powerful mouth
By dragging them one by one down south

Trodding along, doing the best he could
In the muddy muerth he dragged the wood
Then pulled and placed them on his roof
Reinforcing the waterhouse as good as new

Then without hesitation the Beaver went in
To his lodging dam by swimming under
He sat inside eating some berries
Taking it easy until his heart was torn asunder

He smelt a peculiar smell with a twitch
A twitch of his sensitive nose
On the winds and the smell was quaint
The smell of wolves near his burrow

Alarmed, and on edge, he began to tremble
Remembering his friend the fury mouse
He did not know what to do
He did not want them destroying his house

So the Brown Beaver decided to dive
In the water beside his house to stay alive
As the pack of wolves gathered around
His lodging dam waterhouse

He stay hidden down beside the river
In the water as they circled around
As they circled around quite bitter
Because they did not find him in the house

One of the large wolves, a Grey One
The leader of the pack looked to the sky
And howled out loud to the clouds
He was hungry and didn't want to be denied

He stepped forward and turned to his pack
He motioned for them to search the back
But there was nothing for them to attack
The Grey Wolf was angry and react

He stared with piercing eyes into the river
And he noticed nothing important
So he told his pack of wolves
To move along leàving the Beaver dormant

Relieved, tired and definitely afraid
The Brown Beaver stayed awhile and wait
Until the coast cleared and no one neared

To swim underneath into his place

As he sat there he wondered
If and when would the wolves be back?
Would they be back for him again?
This is what he wondered our little friend

But as they rain subsided and clouds parted
The sun came out this afternoon
And he felt better than he did before noon
He decided to venture outside of his room

Into the sunshine and clean air
The Brown Beaver was elated and happy
That the danger was finally gone
But he noticed that something

Something was terribly wrong!
He sensed that something was behind him
As he slowly turned around
He saw the pack of wolves growling

The Brown Beaver started to run
Back to the Chilko River and diving in
The Grey One, gave chase under the sun
Diving into the waters trying to catch him

However, it was to no avail
Our little friend was a better swimmer
And crossed to the other side
Evading the Grey Wolf for his dinner

The Brown Beaver stared back
At the Grey Wolf who never attacked
And the two met with gazing eyes
After that day the wolves never came back

The Brown Beaver was left alone
To live out his life in his quiet home
The world he lived in allowed him to roam
As he once did before his friend the mouse died

But he lived on and on
Building his dam and eating berries

But he never forgot that day
When the pack of wolves came

The day he met the Grey Wolf
And his pack of wolves;
And from that day on
He slept with one eye open
Never to mistake his life or freedom
Ever again.

O.A.

## Take a Chance

On the edge of a ledge
Backs up against a wall
Inches close to jumping
Inches close to the fall
Staring into the abyss
The neverending circus
I see a way out myself
But I might need your help...

Take a chance
And if I'm wrong
I'll move along
And do something else
Take a chance
And if I'm wrong
I'll move along
And do something else

The words are here
In my head and heart
My mind is in the right
But you think my life
Is a sinking ship tonight
But it doesn't have to be
I can work it out you'll see
Don't want to be a casualty

Take a chance
And if I'm wrong
I'll move along
And do something else
Take a chance
And if I'm wrong
I'll move along
And do something else

I can find an audience
I can find an audience
I can find an audience
I can find an audience

One that won't laugh?

That I'm not sure...

Will I embarrass you?
Well I already have...

Take a chance
And if I'm wrong
I'll move along
And do something else.

O.A.

## The Real McCoy System

Elijah McCoy
The Real McCoy
Patented 57 inventions
Quite a few to mention
But the greatest invention
He left his country
Was his last name...

The oil-drip system
That railroad engineers
Would request by name
In North America
Was the basis of his alias
Patented in 1872.

Escaping slavery
In America
His family came to Canada
On the Underground Railroad
In 1842.

My question to you
Might seem overdue
But has there been
A more prolific inventor?
Or someone new
Who has created more
For the railroad boys?

Praises to you, sir,
'The Real Elijah McCoy.'

O.A.

## Loosen the Bonds

Let it go
Let it flow
Loosen the bonds
On this vagabond
On this gypsy man
On this calypso hold
Let it go, let it go, let it go

Loosen the bonds
Before the river dries up
And the water is gone
Loosen the chains
And let this horse ride
Free of the earthly reigns
That reside in my troubled life

They once told me
My trouble is gravity
Loosen the bonds
On this vagabond
On this gypsy man
On this calypso hold
Let it go, let it go, let it go
Oh no, oh no, oh no

Loosen the bonds
Before the river dries up
And the water is gone
Loosen the chains
And let this horse ride
Free of the earthly reigns
That reside in my troubled life

Loosen the bonds
Before the river dries up
And the water is gone
Loosen the chains
And let this horse ride
Free of the earthly reigns
That reside in my troubled life

Time and again

Now and then
I get a glimpse
Of heaven
When I'm allowed to fly
When I'm allowed to fly

So let this bird fly
Free of the earthly reigns
That reside in my troubled life
That reside in my troubled life

F.l.y.
F.l.y.
F.l.y.

O.A.

## The Troll Under the Lions Gate Bridge

I used to dream
Of driving fast
Over the Lions Gate Bridge
To get past
The troll that lived under it

Until one night
I dreamed that I was driving
Over the Lions Gate Bridge
And the troll came up to see me
It climbed the trussels and cables
And stood foot by foot in the road
It was a giant, massive, ugly thing
With pimples, zits and missing teeth
It stood a quite astonishingly 13 feet
And shook the bridge as it walked by
Stopping traffic, as it met my eyes
It opened it's crooked mouth
And then it backed up and spoke:

"You're dreaming! Go back to sleeep!"
"You're dreaming! Go back to sleeep!"
"You're dreaming! Go back to sleeep!"

I used to dream
Of driving fast
Over the Lions Gate Bridge
To get past
The troll that lived under it
The troll that lived under it
The troll that lived under it.

O.A.

## The Grasshopper

From a T.V. Commercial Treatment.

Gazing up at me
Wondering, wondering
Is this man mad?
Or is there a method...

Antennae offset
On the hood of my car
In my garage
In my garage
It stood erect
Mandibles crossed

"Wise ol' grasshopper" I said
I asked out of fear -
"Why do you test me?" I asked
It did not come near -
"I'm only a man here" I answered
It seemed to detest me -

"Wise ol' grasshopper"
I asked out of fear -
"Why do you test me?"
It did not come near -

Gazing up at me
Wondering, wondering
Is this man mad?
Or is there a method...

"Wise ol' grasshopper" I said
I asked out of fear -
"Why do you test me?" I asked
It did not come near -
"I'm only a man here" I answered
It seemed to detest me -

O.A.

**To Stephanie Scott Lloyd**

I read your book: "Philosophical Sayings by a Jamaican" published in 1972.
It is a mystery how we found it, but your book was handed down to me by my Mother.
In the preface, you stated that a columnist of a newspaper mentioned:
No Jamaican has ever written a line worth quoting!
Well in having read your thoughts, and read your lines,
I hope that columnist in 1972 changed his mind.
My favorite poems were: "The Inner Life"
and "Jamaica Comes of Age."
Wherever you are,
I hope you're still writing.

O.A.

## I Aspire to Inspire

These days I aspire to inspire
These days I want anyone I meet
To have a positive experience with me
Not that I was ever rude to begin with
But there's so much negativity
In this unbelievable world
These days

These days I aspire to inspire
These days I want anyone I meet
To have a positive experience with me
When I look into the mirror a good person
Is the catalyst that I plainly see
He is someone I know
Trying to be

Wait to see if the boy in the bubble
Will bring you joy or trouble
Weather the storm
As you did before
Be a golden example
Of right from wrong
Sorry for all the noise
Sorry for all the noise
Be a good girl or boy
In any type of song
That's what I've been
Telling myself all along
Even if your self recollection
Leaves you immune to infection
Basic rights in the suffering light
Is yours to understand every night

Be a golden example
Of right from wrong
Sorry for all the noise
Sorry for all the noise
Be a good girl or boy
In any type of song
That's what I've been
Telling myself all along

These days I aspire to inspire
These days I want anyone I meet
To have a positive experience with me
Not that I was ever rude to begin with
But there's so much negativity
In this unbelievable world
These days

These days I aspire to inspire
These days I want anyone I meet
To have a positive experience with me
When I look into the mirror a good person
Is the catalyst that I plainly see
He is someone I know
Trying to be

Trying to be
In a poem is not easy
Trying to be
In life people call you -
A believer or achiever
There is no middle ground
Any way around
Any way around
All someone can do
Is show that they are down.
Is show that they are down.

These days I aspire to inspire
These days I want anyone I meet
To have a positive experience with me

Words to live by.

O.A.

## A Tribute to Terry Fox

Every year
As people run
To raise money for cancer
To find the answer
To a cure thereafter
As one of Canada's heroes
I did not know
You tried out for the team
And made it through
Playing basketball
With other teammates at SFU!
That's what I call resilient
As you ran across Canada
Raising money for cancer
And did not give up after
When things got tough too
You're an inspiration
To billions Terry Fox
And a real Canadian hero
So thank you.

O.A.

## The Human Condition

In the order of existence
Without being ignorant
The state of human affairs
Is fragile and malignant.

The universe is enormous
Allowing anything to persist
Humans should beware
If aliens should really exist.

O.A.

### "If I Die, Without a Goodbye..."

If I die without saying goodbye,
I hope my death is romanticized
And I walk like Joe Black -
Into my favorite movie,
With an East/West symphony of violins
Castrating my solo organ line...
Like Louis Riel, rebelling
On the final frontier before his time
Of the space beyond eschewed;
Of the space beyond eschewed;
Of the space beyond eschewed;
        Bless me, if I die without rules.

Ii.
Travelling towards the crimson sun
As a dwarfed seraphim, encapsulated
Aglow, abright, reborn, alight -
Along a heavenly conveyor belt
Filled with other cherubs, metamorphosed
From earthly human forms,
That have pierced the sordid skyline
That have pierced the sordid skyline
Bursting through the atmosphere, rocket launched;
And hooking up to the conveyor belt -
Pulling, pulling the skiers up the mountainside
Travelling towards the crimson sun
The earth never looked so distant...
My heavenly passport stamped as: 'one way.'
My angelic capsule is a space-taxi to eternity...

Ili.
I am humbled now
I was fed on earth
I did not starve
I was loved;
If not by many, by someone.
Experimentalists play poker, Theorists play chess.
Theorists always have to be right with their theory.
My theory is that: 'Life can be as brilliant as you want it to be; depending -
On what cards you're dealt. But do not gamble. If it suits you play chess...
If you gamble, understand your hand, and the stakes at hand...
A Queen must always protect a King...

Unless he plays poker.'
My space-taxi has a name:
Her name is - 'Godiva'
'One-way.'

IIIi.
Travelling -
Past the infinite time and space; emptiness:
Blackboard of Physics and Astronomy
Chalking up this outerbody experience
As quintessential to my Eros in Death
And my last life lesson on the Big Bang Theory
Journeying past specs of solar infusion
Journeying past all the space stations
Journeying past the ISS: International Space Station
Wondering if man will ever colonize the moon or mars?

IVi.
As I reach the revolving moon
From my angelic Death Pod being ushered along
Another Dead Soul breaks the eerie silence
By making a historic after-life-thought:
"Look, down there on the moon, a flag!"
I can only peer down with my sad introverted eyes...
Introspectively I was aroused.
Dead and Alive at the same time
Witnessing history, and being shuffled away from it.
Conveyor belt.
Heavenly sent.
Conveyor set.

Godiva closed my pod a little tighter,
Tighter as we all passed by the moon.
I could only believe this was the end
As the beginning and end are one
As the beginning and end are one
The world is a molecule or stem cell
In the creator's head.
Interconnected - round - symmetrical - perfect.
Imperfect is the complex half of perfection.
Introverted eyes feel Godiva's warmth.
Imperfect meets perfection - homeostasis.
Godiva loves everyone I realize...

I am humbled now
I was fed on earth
I did not starve
I was loved;
If not by many, by someone.
>Mantra<

I am humbled now
I was fed on earth
I did not starve
I was loved;
If not by many, by someone.
>Mantra<

I am humbled now
I was fed on earth
I did not starve
I was loved;
If not by many, by someone.
>Mantra<

Vi.
In my lifetime, I have been through alot
But I have bent in the storm
But I have not been broken
Because my loyalty to the divine creature keeps me sane.
I have not been perfect in an imperfect world.
But Godiva now comforts me with her warmth...
The end is near, the beginning is here
The end is near, the beginning is here
Her name is...
Godiva.

As I pass by mercury, I notice red clouds of radiation.
As I pass through a solar wind storm, I notice light particles.
As I pass through an asteroid belt, I notice cosmic friction.
Arriving yet closer to the crimson sun
Godiva turns each seraphim's Death Pod a vibrant green.
Florescent green, for a symbolic sign:
'All systems go.'
Our angelic pods open up and release from the conveyor belt.

Sprouting angel-like wings
We bid farewell to Death

And follow our pod leader 'Godiva'
In a V - shaped pattern
Travelling towards the crimson sun.
I look back at earth to say goodbye
But realize, no one will hear me now...
And turn back around and figure as I wake
Instead of goodbye, I will think of how to say:
"Hello everyone... Sorry I'm late!"

O.A.

Manufactured by Amazon.ca
Bolton, ON

22284860R00069